HAL•LEONARD®
MANDOLIN
PLAY-ALONG

AUDIO
ACCESS
INCLUDED

Italian Classics

T0081562

Mandolin by Mike Butzen

To access audio visit:
www.halleonard.com/mylibrary

Enter Code
6816-5657-1209-6415

ISBN 978-1-4803-4285-9

HAL•LEONARD®
7777 W. BLUEMOUND RD. P.O. BOX 13819 MILWAUKEE, WI 53213

In Australia Contact:
Hal Leonard Australia Pty. Ltd.
4 Lentara Court
Cheltenham, Victoria, 3192 Australia
Email: ausadmin@halleonard.com.au

Visit Hal Leonard Online at
www.halleonard.com

MANDOLIN NOTATION LEGEND

Mandolin music can be notated three different ways: on a *musical staff*, in *tablature*, and in *rhythm slashes*.

RHYTHM SLASHES are written above the staff. Strum chords in the rhythm indicated. Use the chord diagrams found at the top of the first page of the transcription for the appropriate chord voicings.

THE MUSICAL STAFF shows pitches and rhythms and is divided by bar lines into measures. Pitches are named after the first seven letters of the alphabet.

TABLATURE graphically represents the mandolin fretboard. Each of the four horizontal lines represents each of the four courses of strings, and each number represents a fret.

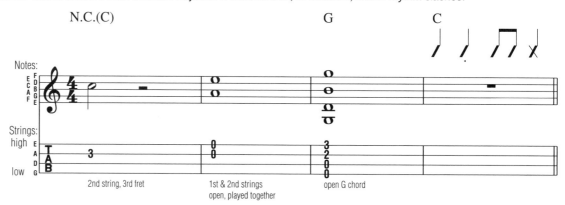

2nd string, 3rd fret   1st & 2nd strings open, played together   open G chord

Definitions for Special Mandolin Notation

MUTED STRING(S): Lightly touch a string with the edge of your fret-hand finger while fretting a note on an adjacent string, causing the muted string to be unheard. Muting all of the strings with the fingers of the fret-hand while strumming the strings with the picking hand produces a percussive effect.

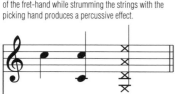

HAMMER-ON: Strike the first (lower) note with one finger, then sound the higher note (on the same string) with another finger by fretting it without picking.

PULL-OFF: Place both fingers on the notes to be sounded. Strike the first note and, without picking, pull the finger off to sound the second (lower) note.

LEGATO SLIDE: Strike the first note and then slide the same fret-hand finger up or down to the second note. The second note is not struck.

SHIFT SLIDE: Same as the legato slide except the second note is struck.

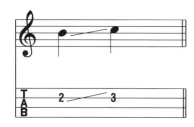

HALF-STEP BEND: Strike the note and bend up ½ step.

GRACE NOTE BEND: Strike the note and immediately bend up as indicated.

TREMOLO PICKING: The note is picked rapidly and continuously.

Additional Musical Definitions

p *(piano)* • Play quietly.

mp *(mezzo-piano)* • Play moderately quiet.

mf *(mezzo-forte)* • Play moderately loud.

f *(forte)* • Play loudly.

cont. rhy. sim. • Continue strumming in similar rhythm.

N.C. *(no chord)* • Don't strum until the next chord symbol. Chord symbols in parentheses reflect implied harmony.

D.S. al Coda • Go back to the sign (𝄋), then play until the measure marked *"To Coda"*, then skip to the section labeled *"Coda."*

D.S.S. al Coda 2 • Go back to the double sign (𝄋𝄋), then play until the measure marked *"To Coda 2"*, then skip to the section labeled *"Coda 2."*

D.S. al Fine • Go back to the sign (𝄋), then play until the label *"Fine."*

 *(staccato)* • Play the note or chord short.

 *(ritard)* • Gradually slow down.

 (fermata) • Hold the note or chord for an undetermined amount of time.

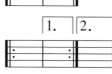 • Repeat measures between signs.

• When a repeated section has different endings, play the first ending only the first time and the second ending only the second time.

NOTE: Tablature numbers in parentheses mean:
1. The note is being sustained over a system (note in standard notation is tied), or
2. The note is sustained, but a new articulation (such as a hammer-on, pull-off or slide) begins.

Italian Classics

Come Back to Sorrento

By Ernesto de Curtis

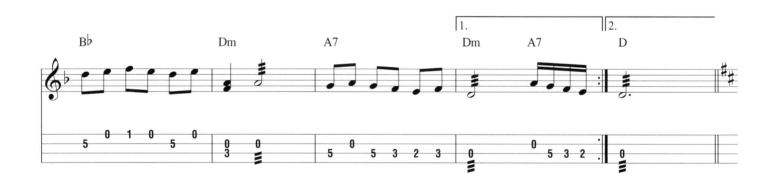

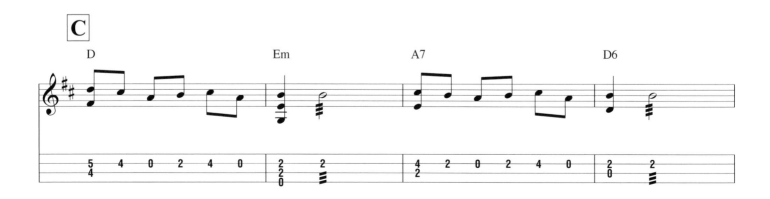

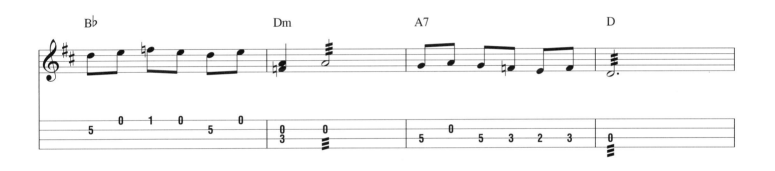

D

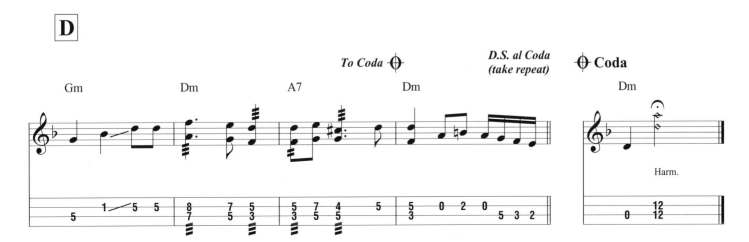

La Spagnola

By Vincenzo Chiari

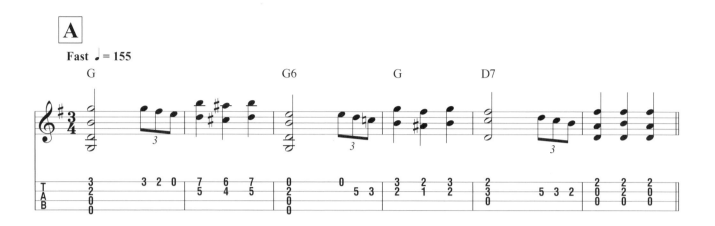

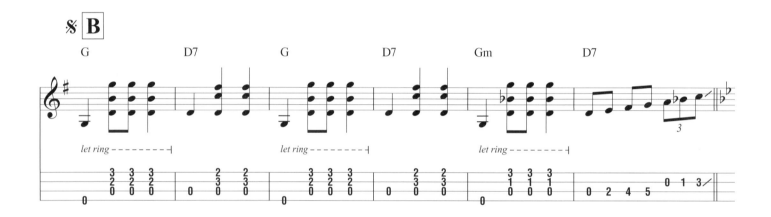

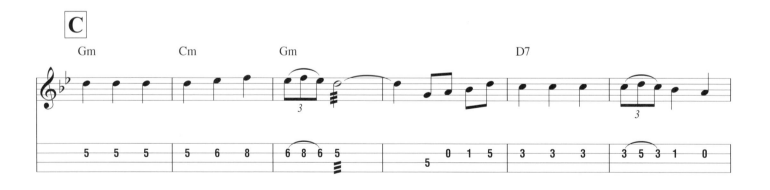

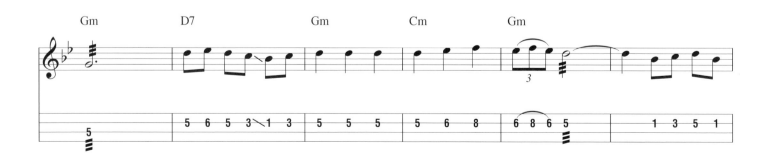

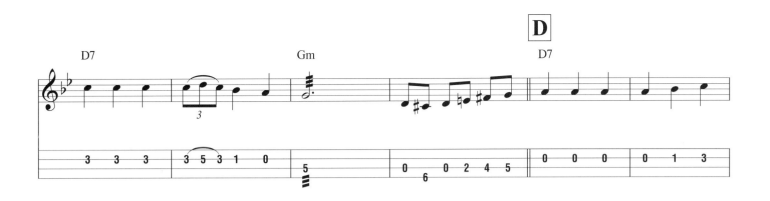

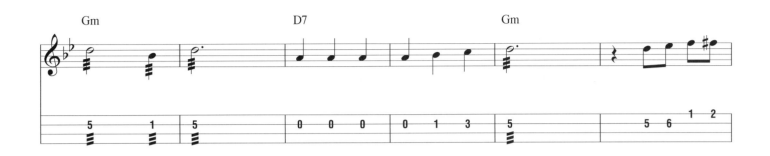

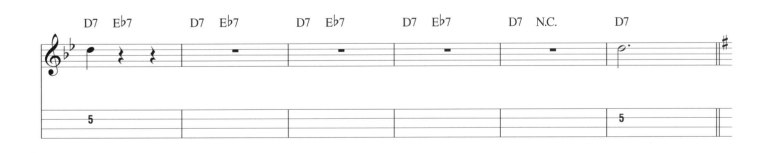

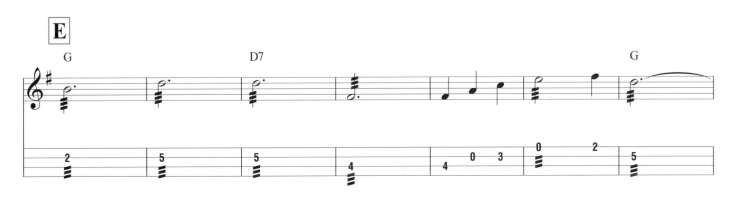

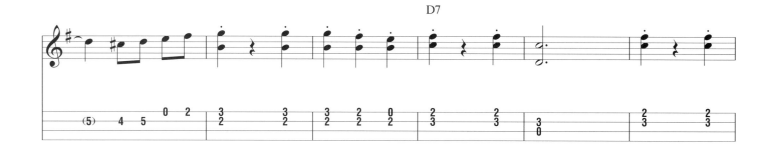

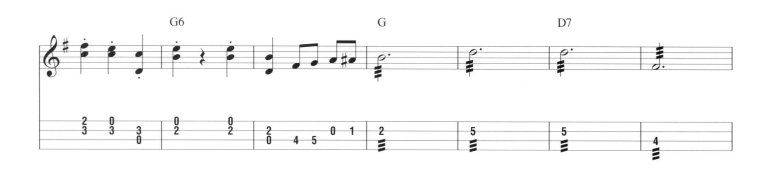

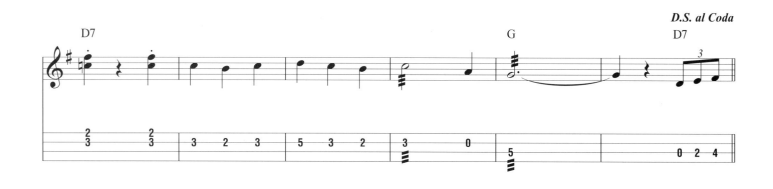

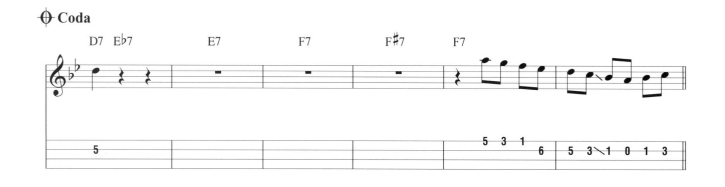

F

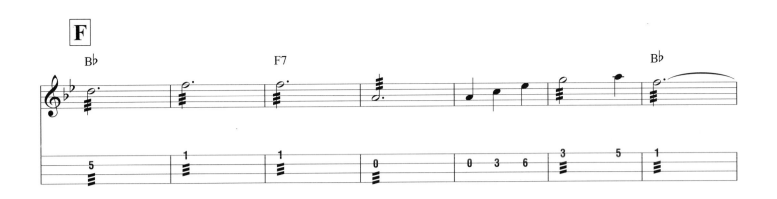

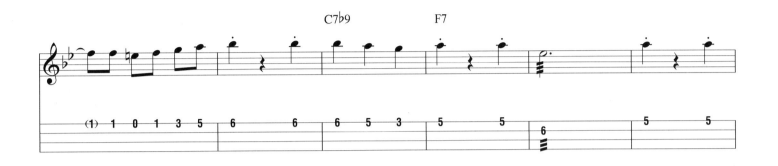

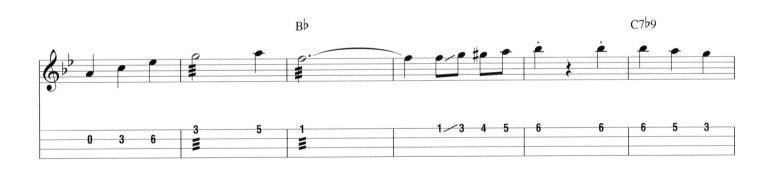

Mattinata

By Ruggero Leoncavallo

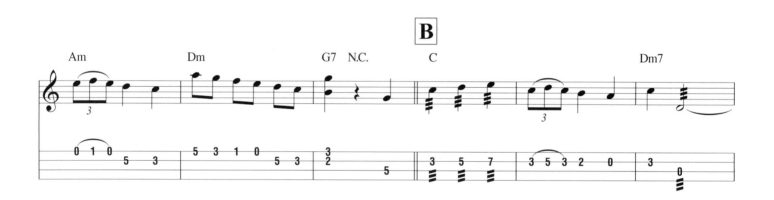

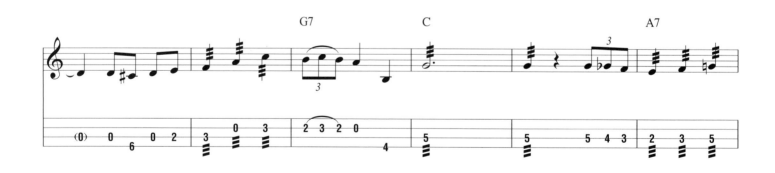

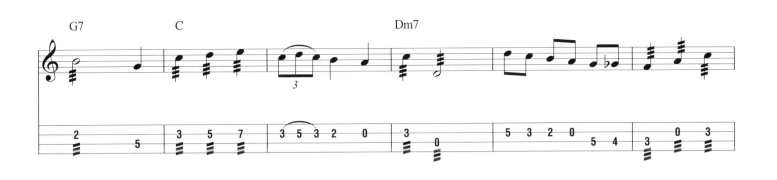

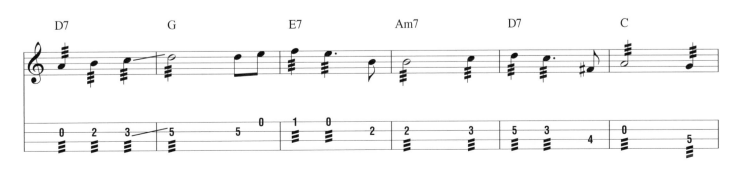

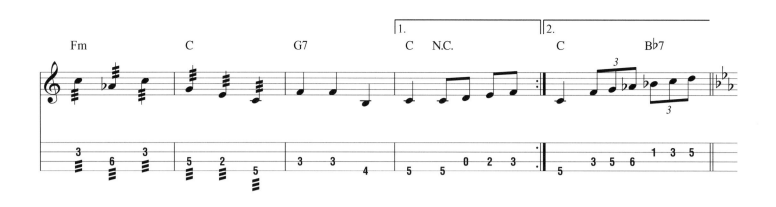

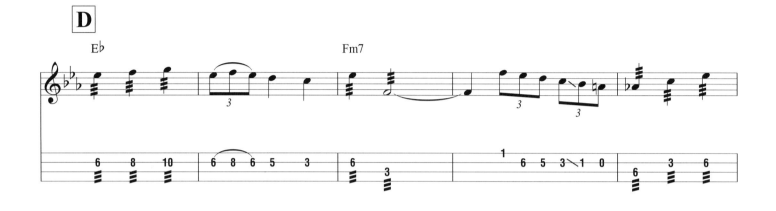

D

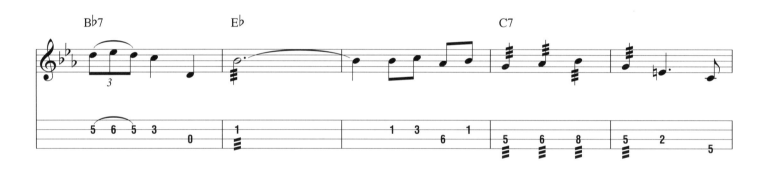

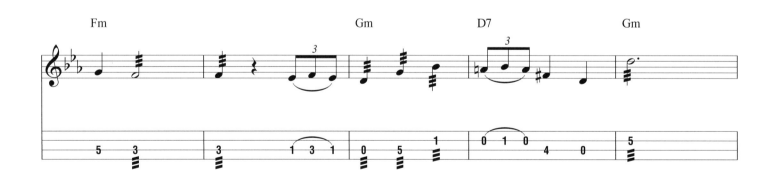

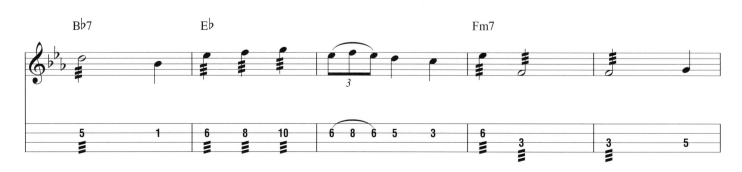

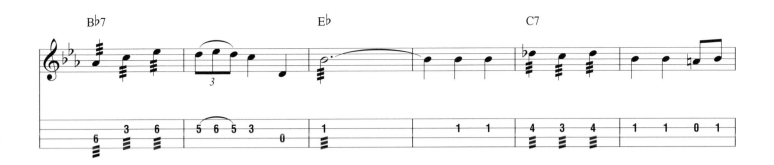

E

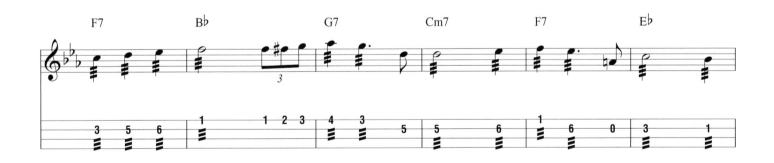

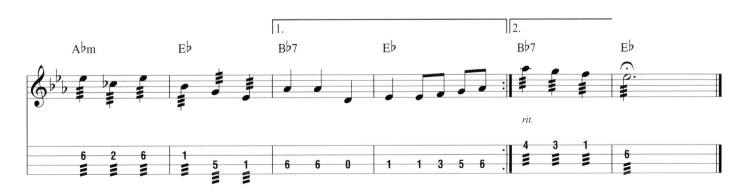

'O Sole Mio

Words by Giovanni Capurro
Music by Eduardo di Capua

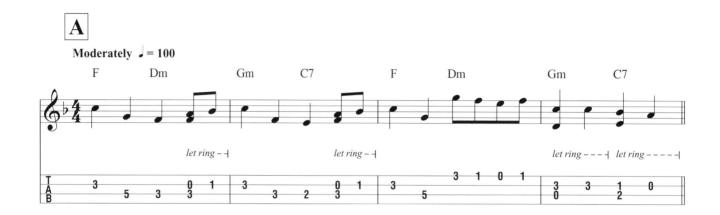

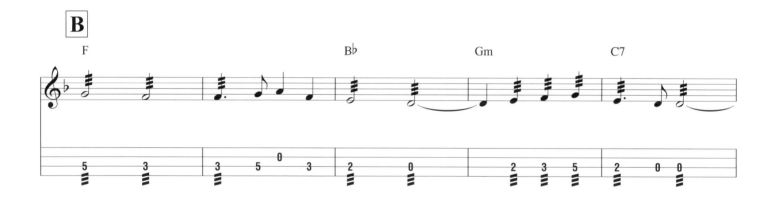

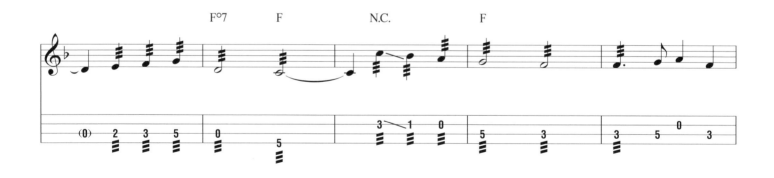

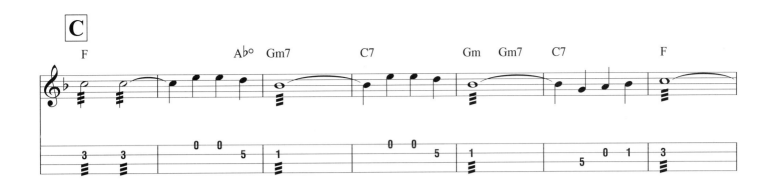

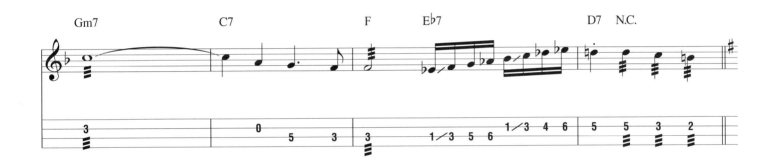

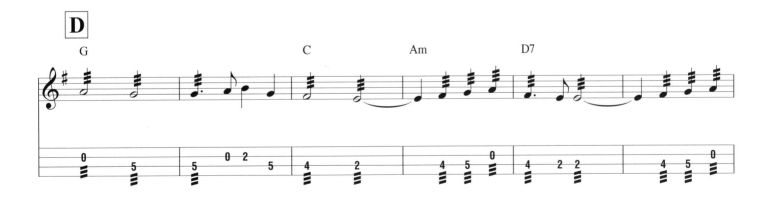

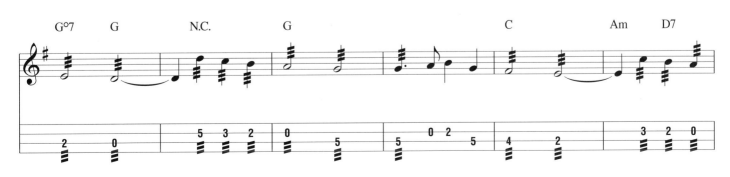

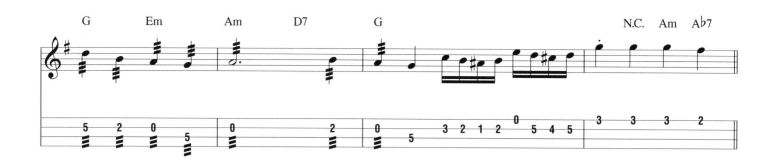

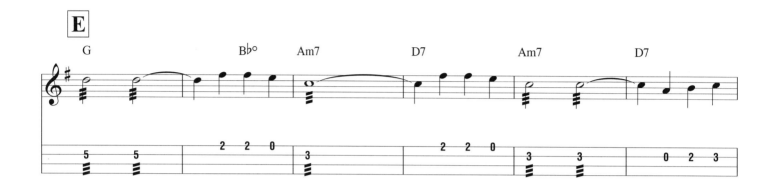

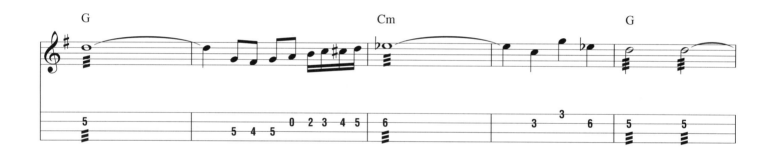

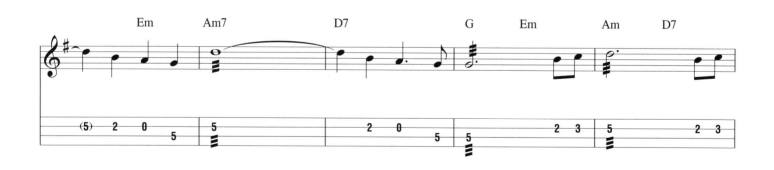

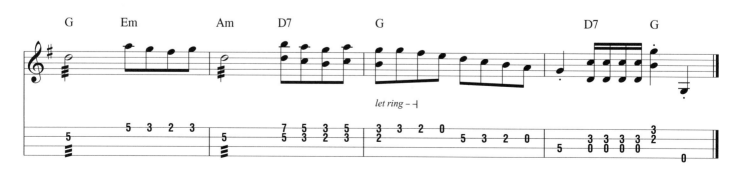

Oh Marie

Words and Music by Eduardo di Capua

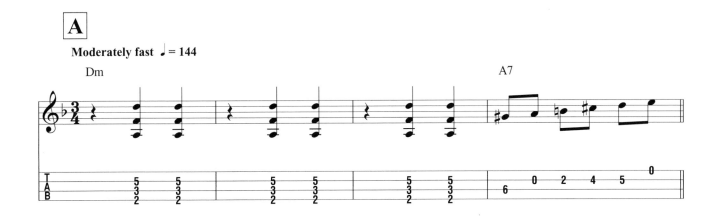

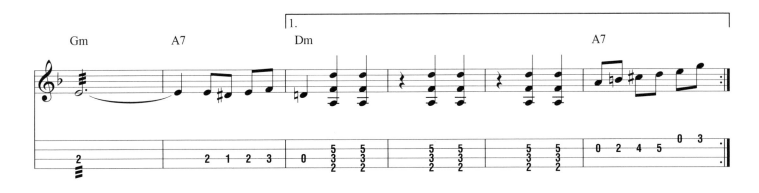

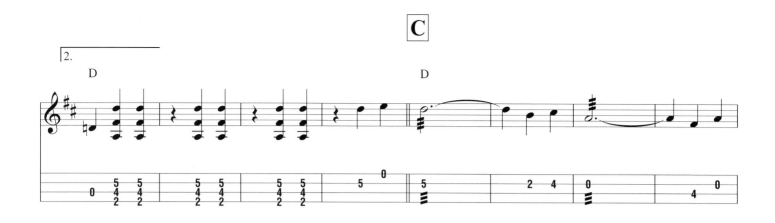

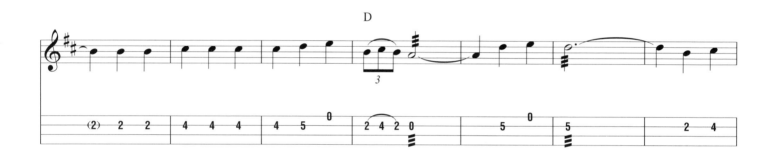

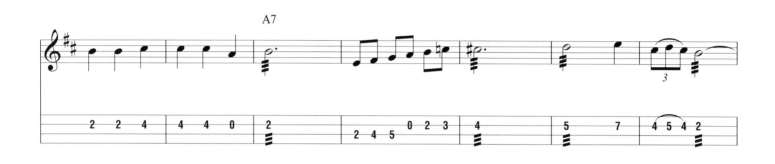

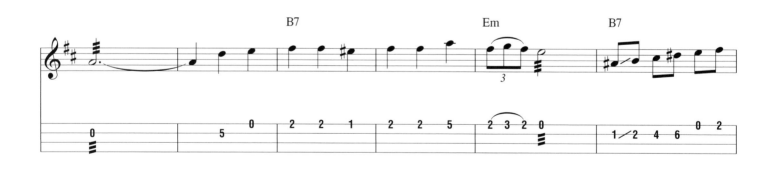

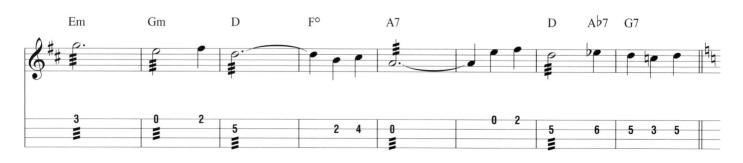

D

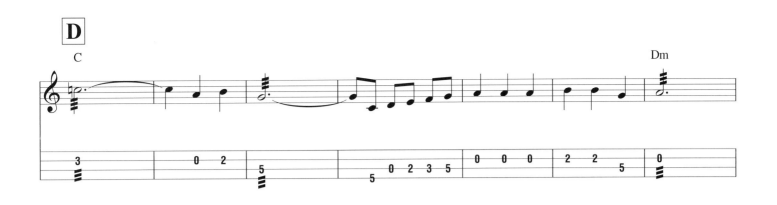

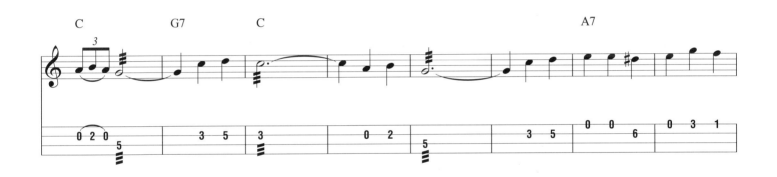

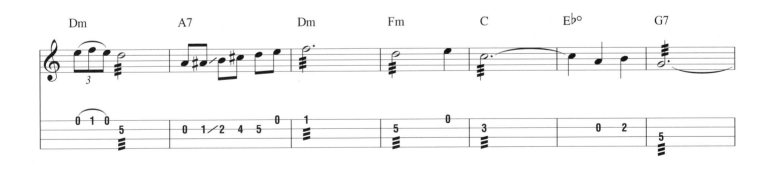

Santa Lucia

By Teodoro Cottrau

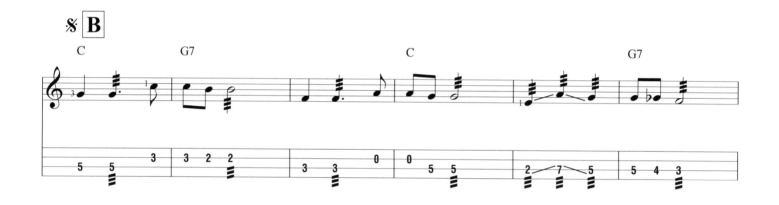

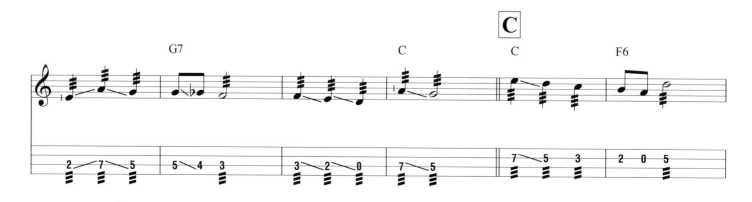

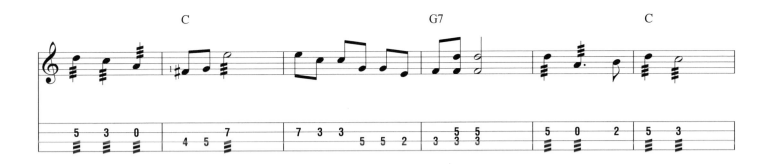

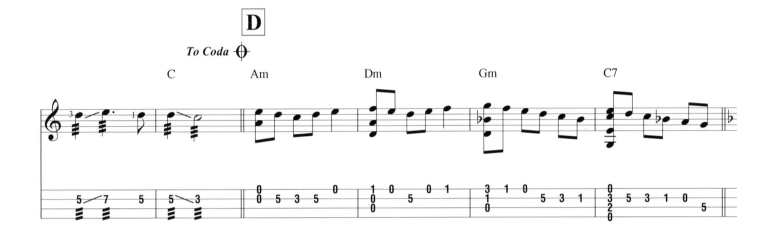

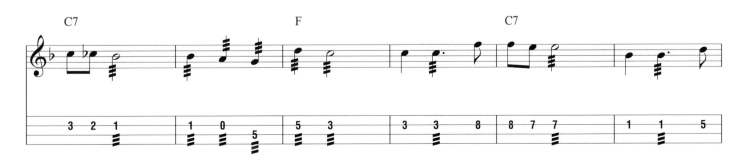

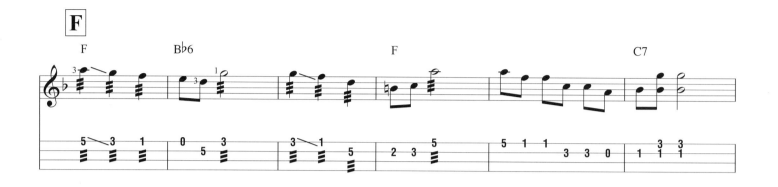

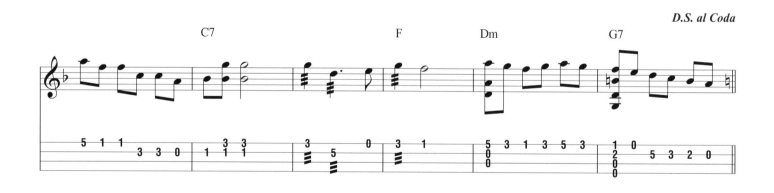

D.S. al Coda

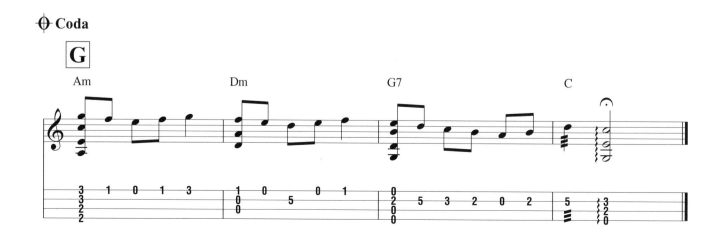

Tarantella

Traditional

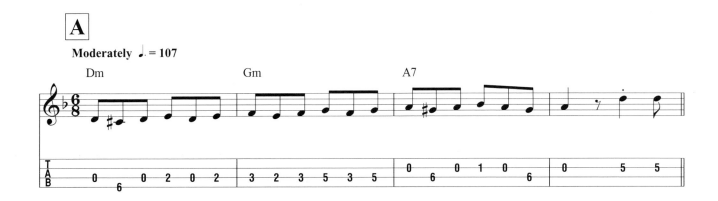

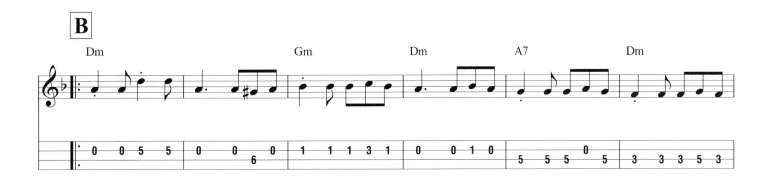

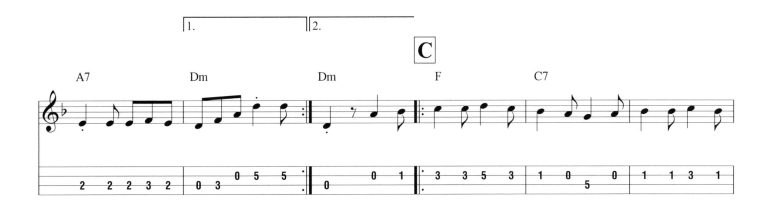

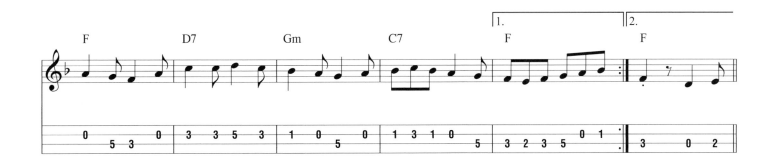

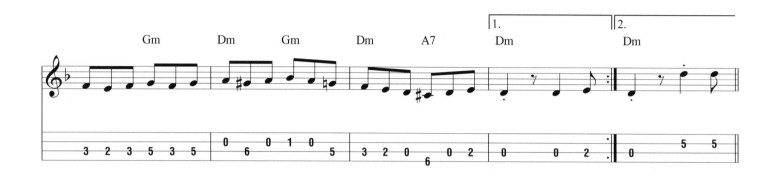

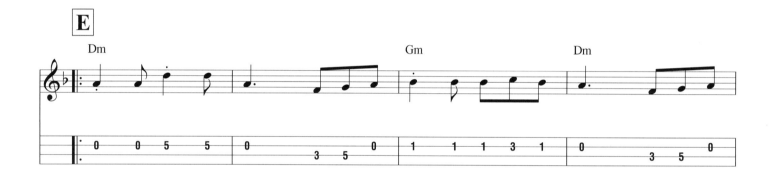

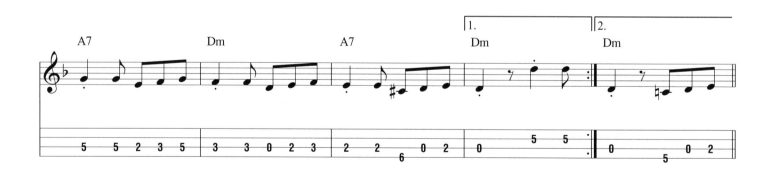

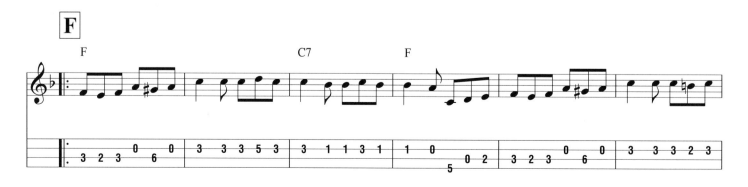

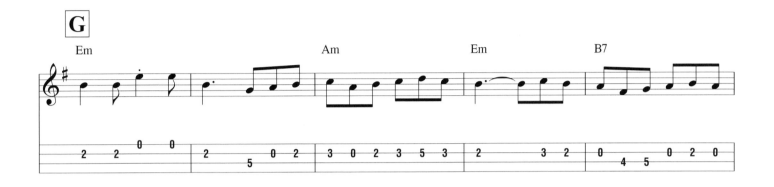

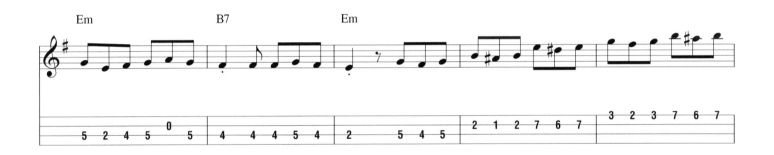

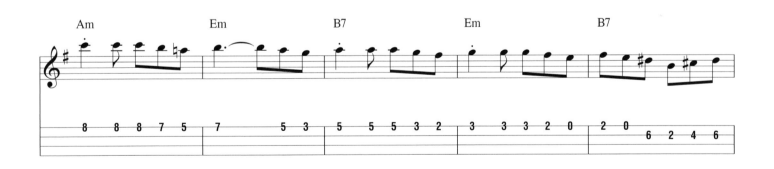

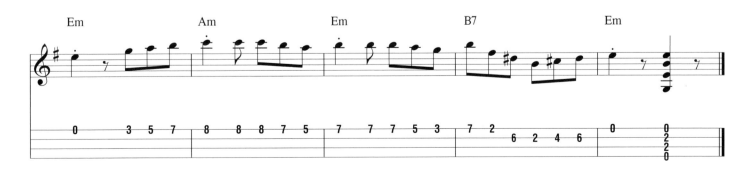

Vieni Sul Mar

Italian Folk Song

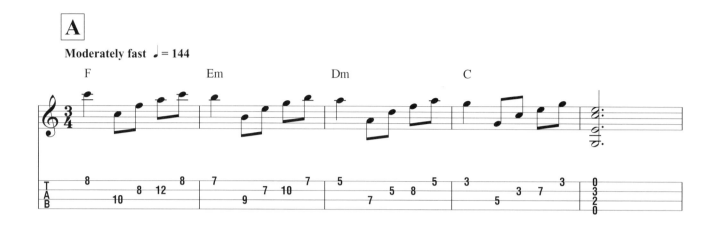

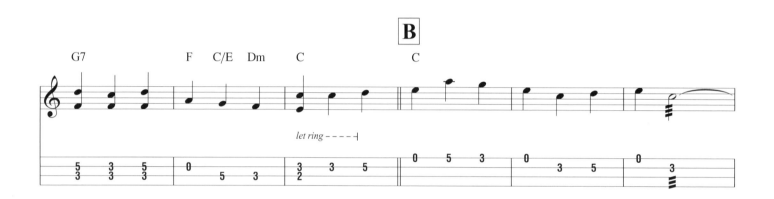

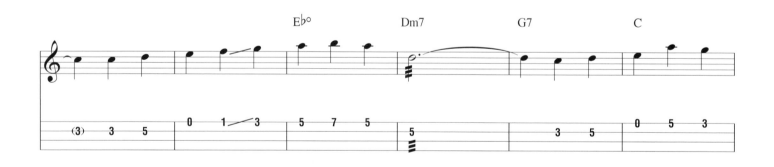

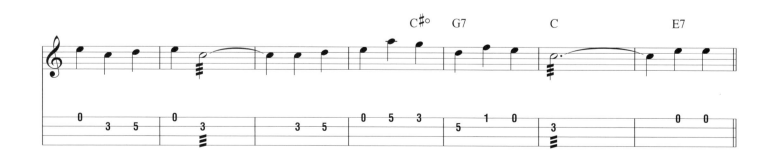

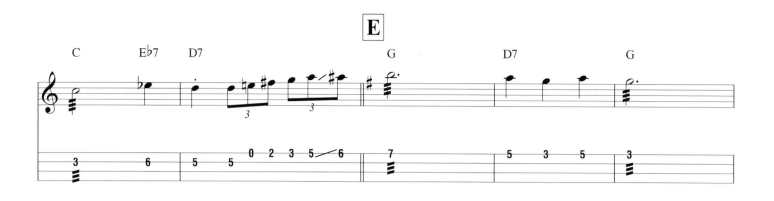

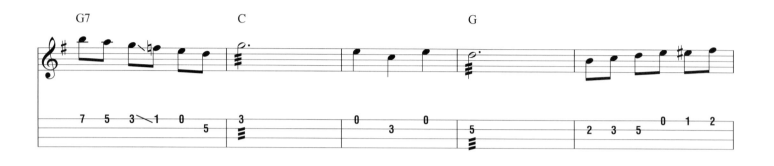

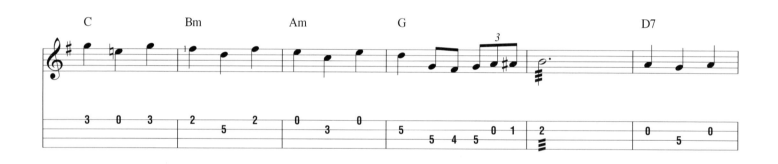

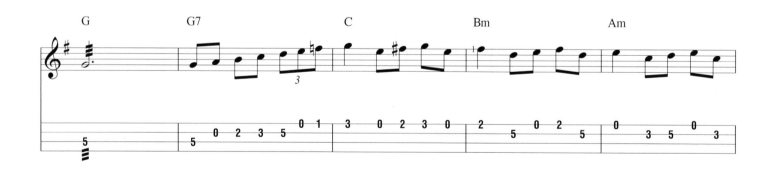

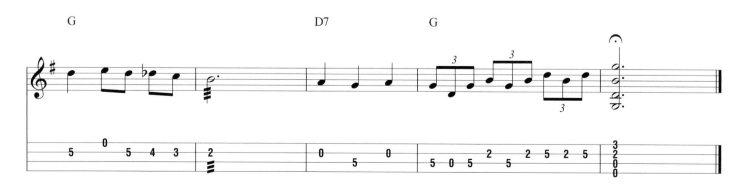

Great Mandolin Publications

from

HAL LEONARD MANDOLIN METHOD

 INCLUDES TAB

Noted mandolinist and teacher Rich Del Grosso has authored this excellent mandolin method that features great playable tunes in several styles (bluegrass, country, folk, blues) in standard music notation and tablature. The optional audio features play-along duets.

00699296 Book Only $7.99
00695102 Book/Online Audio $15.99

EASY SONGS FOR MANDOLIN

SUPPLEMENTARY SONGBOOK TO THE HAL LEONARD MANDOLIN METHOD

20 songs to play as you learn mandolin: Annie's Song • California Dreamin' • Let It Be • Puff the Magic Dragon • Scarborough Fair • Where Have All the Flowers Gone? • and more.

00695865 Book Only $8.99
00695866 Book/CD Pack $15.99

FRETBOARD ROADMAPS – MANDOLIN

 INCLUDES TAB

THE ESSENTIAL PATTERNS THAT ALL THE PROS KNOW AND USE

by Fred Sokolow and Bob Applebaum

The latest installment in our popular Fretboard Roadmaps series is a unique book/CD pack for all mandolin players. The CD includes 48 demonstration tracks for the exercises that will teach players to: play all over the fretboard, in any key; increase their chord, scale and lick vocabulary; play chord-based licks, moveable major and blues scales, first-position major scales and double stops; and more! Includes easy-to-follow diagrams and instructions for all levels of players.

00695357 Book/CD Pack $12.95

MANDOLIN CHORD FINDER

EASY-TO-USE GUIDE TO OVER 1,000 MANDOLIN CHORDS

by Chad Johnson

Learn to play chords on the mandolin with this comprehensive, yet easy-to-use book. The Hal Leonard Mandolin Chord Finder contains over 1,000 chord diagrams for the most important 28 chord types, including three voicings for each chord. Also includes a lesson on chord construction, and a fingerboard chart of the mandolin neck!

00695739 9" X 12" Edition $6.99
00695740 6" X 9" Edition $5.99

MANDOLIN SCALE FINDER

EASY-TO-USE GUIDE TO OVER 1,300 MANDOLIN SCALES

by Chad Johnson

Presents scale diagrams for the most often-used scales and modes in an orderly and easily accessible fashion. Use this book as a reference guide or as the foundation for creating an in-depth practice routine. Includes multiple patterns for each scale, a lesson on scale construction, and a fingerboard chart of the mandolin neck.

00695779 9" X 12" Edition $6.99
00695782 6" X 9" Edition $5.99

BILL MONROE – 16 GEMS

 INCLUDES TAB

Authentic mandolin transcriptions of these classics by the Father of Bluegrass: Blue Grass Breakdown • Blue Grass Special • Can't You Hear Me Calling • Goodbye Old Pal • Heavy Traffic Ahead • I'm Going Back to Old Kentucky • It's Mighty Dark to Travel • Kentucky Waltz • Nobody Loves Me • Old Crossroad Is Waitin' • Remember the Cross • Shine Hallelujah Shine • Summertime Is Past and Gone • Sweetheart You Done Me Wrong • Travelin' This Lonesome Road • True Life Blues.

00690310 Mandolin Transcriptions $12.95

O BROTHER, WHERE ART THOU?

 INCLUDES TAB

Perfect for beginning to advanced players, this collection contains both note-for-note transcribed mandolin solos, as well as mandolin arrangements of the melody lines for 11 songs from this Grammy-winning Album of the Year: Angel Band • The Big Rock Candy Mountain • Down to the River to Pray • I Am a Man of Constant Sorrow • I Am Weary (Let Me Rest) • I'll Fly Away • In the Highways (I'll Be Somewhere Working for My Lord) • In the Jailhouse Now • Indian War Whoop • Keep on the Sunny Side • You Are My Sunshine. Chord diagrams provided for each song match the chords from the original recording, and all songs are in their original key. Includes tab, lyrics and a mandolin notation legend.

00695762 .... $14.99

THE ULTIMATE BLUEGRASS MANDOLIN CONSTRUCTION MANUAL

by Roger H. Siminoff

This is the most complete step-by-step treatise ever written on building an acoustical string instrument. Siminoff, a renowned author and luthier, applies over four decades of experience to guide beginners to pros through detailed chapters on wood selection, cutting, carving, shaping, assembly, inlays, fretting, binding and assembly of an F-style mandolin.

00331088 .... $37.99

Prices, contents and availability are subject to change without notice.

FOR MORE INFORMATION, SEE YOUR LOCAL MUSIC DEALER, OR WRITE TO:

7777 W. BLUEMOUND RD. P.O. BOX 13819 MILWAUKEE, WI 53213

Visit Hal Leonard online at **www.halleonard.com**

0716

Hal Leonard Mandolin Play-Along Series

The Mandolin Play-Along Series will help you play your favorite songs quickly and easily. Just follow the written music, listen to the CD or online audio to hear how the mandolin should sound, and then play along using the separate backing tracks. Standard notation and tablature are both included in the book. The audio is enhanced so users can adjust the recording to any tempo without changing the pitch!

1. BLUEGRASS

Angeline the Baker • Billy in the Low Ground • Blackberry Blossom • Fisher's Hornpipe • Old Joe Clark • Salt Creek • Soldier's Joy • Whiskey Before Breakfast.
00702517 Book/CD Pack....................$14.99

2. CELTIC

A Fig for a Kiss • The Kesh Jig • Morrison's Jig • The Red Haired Boy • Rights of Man • Star of Munster • The Star of the County Down • Temperence Reel.
00702518 Book/CD Pack....................$14.99

3. POP HITS

Brown Eyed Girl • I Shot the Sheriff • In My Life • Mrs. Robinson • Stand by Me • Superstition • Tears in Heaven • You Can't Hurry Love.
00702519 Book/CD Pack....................$14.99

4. J.S. BACH

Bourree in E Minor • Invention No.1 (Bach) • Invention No.2 (Bach) • Jesu, Joy of Man's Desiring • March in D Major • Minuet in G • Musette in D Major • Sleepers, Awake (Wachet Auf).
00702520 Book/CD Pack....................$14.99

5. GYPSY SWING

After You've Gone • Avalon • China Boy • Dark Eyes • Indiana (Back Home Again in Indiana) • Limehouse Blues • The Sheik of Araby • Tiger Rag (Hold That Tiger).
00702521 Book/CD Pack....................$14.99

6. ROCK HITS

Back in the High Life Again • Copperhead Road • Going to California • Ho Hey • Iris • Losing My Religion • Maggie May • Sunny Came Home.
00119367 Book/Online Audio $16.99

7. ITALIAN CLASSICS

Come Back to Sorrento • La Spagnola • Mattinata • 'O Sole Mio • Oh Marie • Santa Lucia • Tarantella • Vieni Sul Mar.
00119368 Book/CD Pack....................$16.99

8. MANDOLIN FAVORITES

Arrivederci Roma (Goodbye to Rome) • The Godfather (Love Theme) • Misirlou • Never on Sunday • Over the Rainbow • Spanish Eyes • That's Amoré (That's Love) • Theme from "Zorba the Greek."
00119494 Book/CD Pack....................$14.99

9. CHRISTMAS CAROLS

Angels We Have Heard on High • Carol of the Bells • Go, Tell It on the Mountain • Hark! the Herald Angels Sing • Joy to the World • O Holy Night • Silent Night • We Wish You a Merry Christmas.
00119895 Book/CD Pack....................$14.99

11. CLASSICAL THEMES

Blue Danube Waltz • Eine Kleine Nachtmusik ("Serenade"), First Movement Excerpt • Für Elise • Humoresque • In the Hall of the Mountain King • La donna e mobile • The Merry Widow Waltz • Spring, First Movement.
00156777 Book/Online Audio $14.99

HAL•LEONARD®
CORPORATION
7777 W. BLUEMOUND RD. P.O. BOX 13819
MILWAUKEE, WISCONSIN 53213

www.halleonard.com

Prices, contents, and availability subject to change without notice.

0416

101 TIPS FROM HAL LEONARD

STUFF ALL THE PROS KNOW AND USE

Ready to take your skills to the next level? These books present valuable how-to insight that musicians of all styles and levels can benefit from. The text, photos, music, diagrams and accompanying audio provide a terrific, easy-to-use resource for a variety of topics.

101 HAMMOND B-3 TIPS
by Brian Charette
Topics include: funky scales and modes; unconventional harmonies; creative chord voicings; cool drawbar settings; ear-grabbing special effects; professional gigging advice; practicing effectively; making good use of the pedals; and much more!
00128918 Book/Online Audio $14.99

101 HARMONICA TIPS
by Steve Cohen
Topics include: techniques, position playing, soloing, accompaniment, the blues, equipment, performance, maintenance, and much more!
00821040 Book/CD Pack..................................$16.99

101 CELLO TIPS—2ND EDITION
by Angela Schmidt
Topics include: bowing techniques, non-classical playing, electric cellos, accessories, gig tips, practicing, recording and much more!
00149094 Book/Online Audio $14.99

101 FLUTE TIPS
by Elaine Schmidt
Topics include: selecting the right flute for you, finding the right teacher, warm-up exercises, practicing effectively, taking good care of your flute, gigging advice, staying and playing healthy, and much more.
00119883 Book/CD Pack..................................$14.99

101 SAXOPHONE TIPS
by Eric Morones
Topics include: techniques; maintenance; equipment; practicing; recording; performance; and much more!
00311082 Book/CD Pack..................................$14.95

101 SINGING TIPS
by Adam St. James
Topics include: vocal exercises, breathing exercises, the singer's health, preparation, technique, understanding music, singing harmony, microphones, career advice, and much more!
00740308 Book/CD Pack..................................$14.95

101 TRUMPET TIPS
by Scott Barnard
Topics include: techniques, articulation, tone production, soloing, exercises, special effects, equipment, performance, maintenance and much more.
00312082 Book/CD Pack..................................$14.99

101 UPRIGHT BASS TIPS
by Andy McKee
Topics include: right- and left-hand technique, improvising and soloing, practicing, proper care of the instrument, ear training, performance, and much more.
00102009 Book/Online Audio $14.99

101 BASS TIPS
by Gary Willis
Topics include: techniques, improvising and soloing, equipment, practicing, ear training, performance, theory, and much more.
00695542 Book/Online Audio $16.95

101 DRUM TIPS—2ND EDITION
by Scott Schroedl
Topics include: grooves, practicing, warming up, tuning, gear, performance, and much more!
00151936 Book/Online Audio $14.99

101 FIVE-STRING BANJO TIPS
by Fred Sokolow
Topics include: techniques, ear training, performance, and much more!
00696647 Book/CD Pack..................................$14.99

101 GUITAR TIPS
by Adam St. James
Topics include: scales, music theory, truss rod adjustments, proper recording studio set-ups, and much more. The book also features snippets of advice from some of the most celebrated guitarists and producers in the music business.
00695737 Book/Online Audio $16.95

101 MANDOLIN TIPS
by Fred Sokolow
Topics include: playing tips, practicing tips, accessories, mandolin history and lore, practical music theory, and much more!
00119493 Book/Online Audio $14.99

101 RECORDING TIPS
by Adam St. James
This book contains recording tips, suggestions, and advice learned firsthand from legendary producers, engineers, and artists. These tricks of the trade will improve anyone's home or pro studio recordings.
00311035 Book/CD Pack..................................$14.95

101 UKULELE TIPS
by Fred Sokolow with Ronny Schiff
Topics include: techniques, improvising and soloing, equipment, practicing, ear training, performance, uke history and lore, and much more!
00696596 Book/Online Audio $14.99

101 VIOLIN TIPS
by Angela Schmidt
Topics include: bowing techniques, non-classical playing, electric violins, accessories, gig tips, practicing, recording, and much more!
00842672 Book/CD Pack..................................$14.99

Prices, contents and availability subject to change without notice.

HAL•LEONARD® CORPORATION
7777 W. BLUEMOUND RD. P.O. BOX 13819 MILWAUKEE, WI 53213
www.halleonard.com

1215